EGMONT

We bring stories to life

First published in Great Britain in 2007
by Egmont UK Limited
239 Kensington High Street, London W8 6SA

© Hergé/Moulinsart 2007

The authors would like to thank Valerie Van De Weghe
for her translation of *Flight 714 to Sydney*.

ISBN 978 1 4052 3359 0

1 3 5 7 9 10 8 6 4 2

Printed in Belgium

Note to parents: adult supervision is recommended
when sharp-pointed items such as scissors are in use.

TINTIN
& SNOWY

album **3**

Conceived, designed and written by Guy Harvey and Simon Beecroft
in collaboration with Studio Moulinsart

EGMONT

Contents

Off We Go!

Just like Tintin, you're off
on an adventure. Turn the pages
and you will travel to far-flung places,
solve mind-boggling puzzles and
quizzes, discover how aeroplanes work,
and learn how to make spooky
shrunken heads! Get ready to jump
into the action – and have fun!

Young Friends

Tintin travels all around the world having adventures. Along the way, he outwits many devious criminals and meets many interesting people, young and old. Here are some of the young people he's met on his travels.

Zorrino

Nationality: Peruvian (from Peru, in South America)
Occupation: Orange-seller
Characteristics: Brave, loyal, resourceful
How he helps Tintin: Guides him to the Temple of the Sun to rescue Professor Calculus
Why he helps Tintin: Tintin rescues him from a pair of bullies who kick his basket of oranges

Miarka

Who is she? A Romany gypsy
Where does she live? Her family travels around in caravans
Characteristics: Adventurous, feisty, easily upset
How she meets Tintin: She is lost in the woods near Marlinspike Hall; Tintin helps her back to her family

Coco

Nationality: Congolese (from the Congo, in Africa)
Occupation: Guide
Characteristics: Friendly, unlucky, an excellent cook
How he meets Tintin: Tintin needs a guide when he arrives in the Congo
What happens: He and Tintin have several adventures: Tintin's car is stolen, then the thief is captured (but escapes), and finally Tintin wrecks (and mends) a train!

Lobsang

Nationality: Tibetan (from Tibet, in Asia)
Occupation: Novice (apprentice) monk
Characteristics: Active (likes walking), afraid of dogs that bite his robe, fit (runs fast to get away from Snowy!)
How he meets Tintin: He doesn't – he meets Snowy
What happens: Snowy bites the edge of his robe to get his attention – trying to let him know that Tintin is stranded on the mountain with a twisted ankle
Says: "A mad dog! Help!"

Abdullah

Surname: Kalish Ezab
Nationality: Khemedian
(from a fictitious Arabian country called Khemed)
Family: Son of Ben Kalish Ezab, the Emir of Khemed
Characteristics: Spoilt, mischievous, hyperactive
How he meets Tintin: Tintin rescues Abdullah twice
(in *Land of Black Gold* and *The Red Sea Sharks*).
He even lived at Marlinspike Hall for a while!
Likes: Playing practical tricks on Captain Haddock
Hates: Being told "no"!

Chang

Surname: Chong-chen
Nationality: Chinese
Characteristics: Clever, friendly, courageous
Who is he? A young orphan who Tintin saves from drowning (in *The Blue Lotus*); Tintin's dearest friend
Age when first meets Tintin: 10
Age when next meets Tintin: About 15 (in *Tintin In Tibet*, when Tintin rescues him after a plane crash in the Himalayas)
Adopted parent: Wang Chen-yee, another loyal friend of Tintin

Picture Stories

Georges Rémi, famously known as Hergé, is the artist who created, drew and wrote all the Tintin adventures. He chose to tell each adventure as a comic strip. Comic strips use pictures and words to tell the story. A comic strip artist employs lots of special techniques to make the story exciting and believable. Here we are going to look at some of the clever methods that Hergé used to make his stories so entertaining to read and to look at.

Speed lines are a simple way of showing that a vehicle, person or object is moving.

Widescreen

The shape and size of a single picture can create a powerful effect. In the wide frame used here, Tintin and Haddock are tiny figures in a huge, empty desert.

Suspense

Hergé creates suspense by letting us see something that Tintin does not. Here, we are immediately fearful because we can see that Tintin is about to get ambushed.

That night...

Indicators

Sometimes we need to know when or where a scene takes place. Hergé uses indicators like "That night ..."

Action Scene

One of Hergé's favourite tricks is to show action in a single panel. Looking from left to right, we can see the gunmen reacting to Haddock's shouts, getting up, and running away. We see time passing within a single picture. Very neat!

Sub-Plots

The plot is the main story. A sub-plot is a story that happens within the main story. Hergé's sub-plots are often about funny things that Snowy does.

All in the Mind

When we read a Tintin story, we see everything that happens as if we were an observer. But sometimes, we see something that only another character sees, as when Haddock sees Tintin turn into a bottle!

Sound Effects

Hergé creates sound effects in many ways. One of them is to draw stars and a swirl above a character. We know the stars are not really there, but we understand it means "crash!"

The Tintin Test

Test your knowledge of Tintin's adventures. The four sections cover different aspects of Tintin's world. (Answers on page 68)

Part 1: Tintin

1 In which adventure does Tintin recover the Arumbaya Fetish, stolen from a museum?

    A *Cigars of the Pharaoh*
    B *The Broken Ear*
    C *The Seven Crystal Balls*

2 In the picture, where is Tintin about to land?

    A In the sea
    B On an aeroplane
    C On a meteorite

3 What phrase does Tintin use?

    A Wowie zowie
    B Blimey
    C Great snakes!

Part 2: Snowy

1 Who is Snowy's sometime animal rival at Marlinspike Hall?

    A Bianca Castafiore's parrot
    B A magpie
    C A Siamese cat

2 How does Snowy bark?

    A Wooah!
    B Woof
    C Bow wow

3 What unfortunate habit does Snowy share with Captain Haddock?

    A Pipe smoking
    B Whisky drinking
    C Bone chewing

4 In which of these pictures has Snowy dug up the oldest bone?

A   B   C   D

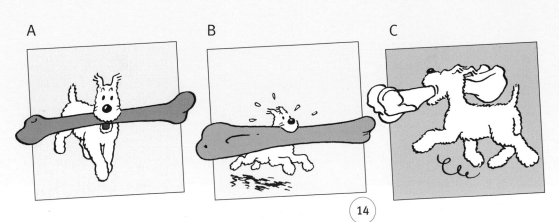
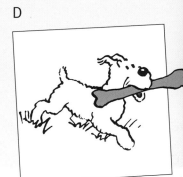

Part 3: Crooks in America

1 Which famous gangster does Tintin meet in America?

A Al Capone
B Machine Gun Kelly
C Baby Face Nelson

2 How does Tintin avoid a peppering from machine gun fire?

A Runs away
B Fast dancing
C Uses a dummy

3 What do the initials G.S.C. stand for?

A Great Society of Criminals
B Guns, Shootings and Crime
C Gangsters' Syndicate of Chicago

4 Which picture does NOT show an American gangster?

A

B

C

D

Part 4: Transport

1 What form of transport does Tintin take when he finally leaves America?

A Aeroplane
B Hot air balloon
C Ocean liner

2 How does Tintin reach the meteorite island in *The Shooting Star*?

A Rowing boat
B Rubber dinghy
C Seaplane

3 What animal does Captain Haddock ride at Marlinspike Hall?

A A llama
B A donkey
C A horse

4 What is the name of the ship, shown below, that helps Tintin in *The Red Sea Sharks*?

A USS Los Angeles
B USS Mississippi
C USS Alabama

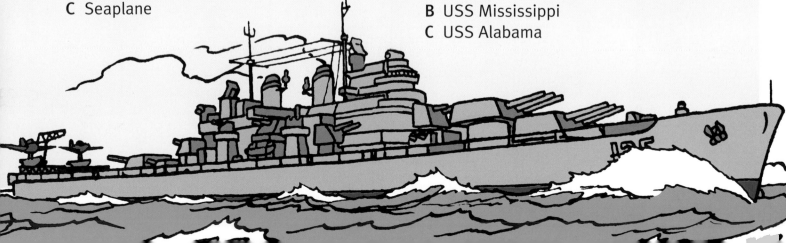

Animals and Owners

Tintin has a head for puzzles. He enjoys the challenge of looking for answers in random clues. That's why he's a great investigator! In this puzzle, four characters each own a different animal. Using the three clues and your powers of logical thinking, see if you can work out who has which animal.

Use the grid to help you.

Check whether you are right on page 68.

Clues

- The shopkeeper's animal can't fly
- Max's animal has hair, so does the captain's
- The captain's animal doesn't bark

The shopkeeper	The captain	Max	Alonso

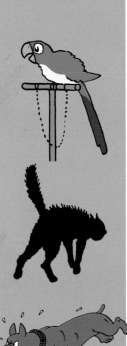

Jungle Jumble

Tintin and General Alcazar are
in the South American jungle.
This word search is like a jungle.
Can you see the words hiding in it?

G	O	S	P	O	R	E	S	T	I	H
C	A	R	N	I	V	A	L	A	T	A
A	L	T	H	O	J	E	W	S	H	D
L	P	S	S	I	W	B	A	M	O	D
C	X	E	J	P	M	Y	L	N	M	O
U	T	P	G	T	O	Y	C	U	P	C
L	I	D	E	G	Y	N	A	P	S	K
U	N	L	Q	U	Y	E	Z	Y	O	N
S	T	A	P	I	O	C	A	R	N	W
T	I	R	E	J	F	W	R	A	S	C
E	N	M	J	U	N	G	L	E	W	E
C	A	S	T	A	F	I	O	R	E	P

Alcazar   Tintin   Peggy
Tapioca   Snowy   Thompsons
Jungle   Calculus   Haddock
Castafiore   Carnival   Sponz

(Answers on page 68)

Signalling Flags

International code flags are used to signal between two ships or between a ship and the shore. Each signalling flag has a different colour, shape or marking which can be used singly or in combination to communicate different messages.

1

Keep Away!

The Pachacamac is running a yellow flag and a yellow and blue pennant – meaning infectious disease on board.

One-Flag Signals

One-flag signals are urgent and have standard meanings.

F
I am disabled – please communicate

G
I need a pilot

A
Diver down – keep well clear

H
I have a pilot on board

B
Dangerous cargo

I
Altering course to port

C
Yes

J
On fire – keep clear

D
Keep clear – manoeuvring with difficulty

K
I wish to communicate with you

E
Altering course to starboard

L
In port – quarantine
At sea – stop instantly

M
I am stopped

N
No

O
Man overboard

P
About to sail

Q
Request clearance to enter port

R
(No meaning in flag code)

S
Engines going astern

T
Keep clear

U
You are running into danger

V
I require assistance

W
I require medical assistance

X
Stop – and watch for my signals

Y
I am dragging my anchor

Z
I require a tug

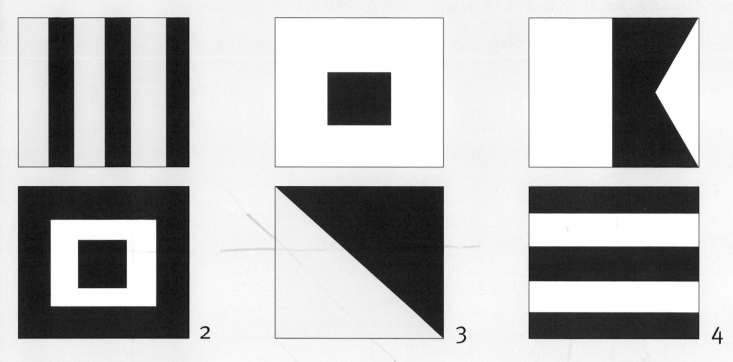

Two-Flag Signals

Sometimes ships fly two flags above one another to give specific meanings. For example, the "A" flag above the "N" flag means "I need a doctor". Can you decode the four examples shown above? Choose four from the list of meanings shown on the right.

(Answers on page 68)

When flags are combined, the meaning can be very different from the one-flag signals. Here are some common examples:

A and C   I am abandoning my vessel.
A and N   I need a doctor.
B and R   I need a helicopter.
G and W   Man overboard. Please pick him up.
S and O   You should stop your vessel immediately.
U and M   The harbour is closed to traffic.
Z and L   Your signal is received but not understood.

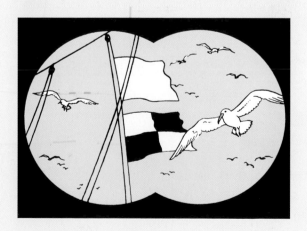

Quarantine

As Captain Haddock can see, a yellow flag and a yellow and black chequered flag means a ship is in quarantine. The ship won't be able to dock until it can show a clean bill of health to the port authorities.

The Wild West

Yee-hah! It's a cowboy's life for Tintin, with his cowboy hat and trousers. But it's not all gunslinging and rodeos for real cowboys. It's a hard, tough life that requires great skill and determination. Let's find out some more about cowboys and the Wild West.

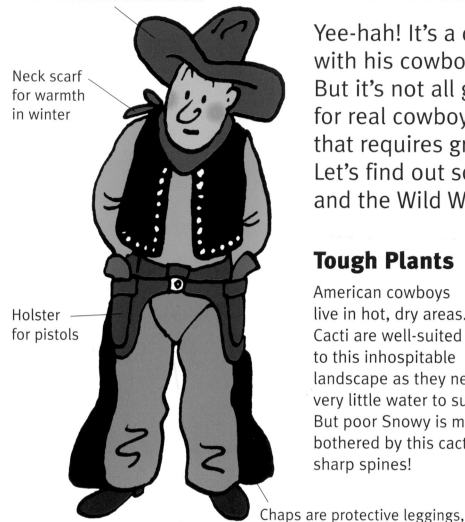

Wide-brimmed hat is both an umbrella and a sun shade

Neck scarf for warmth in winter

Holster for pistols

Chaps are protective leggings, usually made of leather

Tough Plants

American cowboys live in hot, dry areas. Cacti are well-suited to this inhospitable landscape as they need very little water to survive. But poor Snowy is more bothered by this cactus's sharp spines!

A Cowboy's Life

Cowboys look after cattle and horses on ranches. They feed the animals, brand or mark them, and tend to their injuries or other needs. They also take the animals to market.

Railways

The railways connected the remote West America to the rest of the continent. They also carried money from one place to another, so became targets for bandits, who would blow up the safe with dynamite. With vast, empty desert all around, the robbers could then easily escape and not be found.

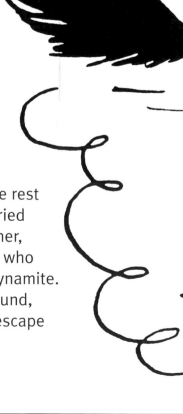

Harsh Justice

In the old Wild West, law and order was a rough and ready affair. Ordinary people often took the law into their own hands. Lynch mobs would decide whom to hang, and more often than not the victim was innocent – as Tintin is.

The lynching of Tintin draws a crowd.

The Sheriff in the part of the Wild West that Tintin visits is more fond of whisky than keeping the peace!

Horse's head harness is called a bridle

Horse Riders

Cowboys are expert horse riders. They show off their skills at rodeos. At first, working cowboys took part in rodeos for entertainment. Now, professional performers make a living at rodeos and do not work on ranches as cowboys.

Lasso has a loop at one end through which the other end runs

Cowboys live on the land and are experienced at looking after themselves in often difficult times. Tintin is just the same – he's a born survivor.

Snowy won't let a mere horse beat him!

Moon Missions

Ground Control to Rocket – first we need your help to orbit the moon. Then we need a brave volunteer to enter a dark Moon cavern and explore ghostly hanging rock formations. Message understood?

1 Ask an adult to open out the coat hanger so you have a long strip of wire. Cut a strip that measures 10 cm longer than the straw length. Insert the wire into the straw and bend the wire as shown, taking care not to damage the straw.

Coat hanger wire

2 Trace the picture of Calculus's Rocket (above) on to a piece of card. Cut it out and colour it in. Open out the paper clip and tape the Rocket to one end. Tape the other end of the wire on to the outside of the straw.

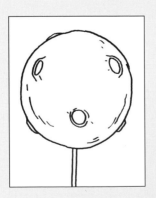

3 To make the Moon, roll the plasticine into a ball about 5 cm in diameter. Mould some craters on to the surface and paint it, if you wish. Carefully stick the Moon on to the end of the wire.

4 To make the Rocket orbit the Moon, hold the wire at one end (A) and with your other hand twist the Straw (B).

A   B

Orbiting Rocket

Watch the Moon Rocket travel around the Moon in this incredible moving model. It's simple to make, but very exciting to watch it turn.

You Will Need

- Length of wire (for example, a coat hanger)
- Paper clip
- Bendy straw
- Plasticine
- Sticky tape
- Scissors
- Paints and pens
- Tracing paper
- Card

Unfolded paper clip

Bend the paper clip wire so it curves around the Moon.

Paint the straw if you want to!

Strange Rocks

On the Moon, Tintin finds stalactites in a cave. Scientists in the real world have not found stalactites on the Moon, but these icicle-shaped rocks form in many caves on Earth. Water drips through the ceiling, leaving behind minerals before it falls. The splash on the floor can also cause upward-pointing stalagmites to grow.

Grow a Stalactite

Watch mini-stalactites grow before your eyes with this amazing science experiment. You might even see some stalagmites forming as well. But you'll have to be patient, as they grow very slowly over several days.

You Will Need

- Two plastic jars (or any containers)
- 30–60 cm thick cotton or string
- Epsom Salts (available from chemists; as an alternative, you could use baking soda, or household salt)
- Hot water
- Washers or weights
- Small plate

1 Fill a jar with the Epsom salts. Then fill to the same level with hot water, or until no more salts will dissolve. Repeat with other jar.

Epsom salts

Epsom salts dissolved in water

2 If the string is thin, double it over and twist it. Attach weights to each end of the string and put each end into one of the jars.

3 Set up the jars and plate as shown below, in a draught-free area. The string may need to be wet beforehand. The stalactites will take a few days to start forming.

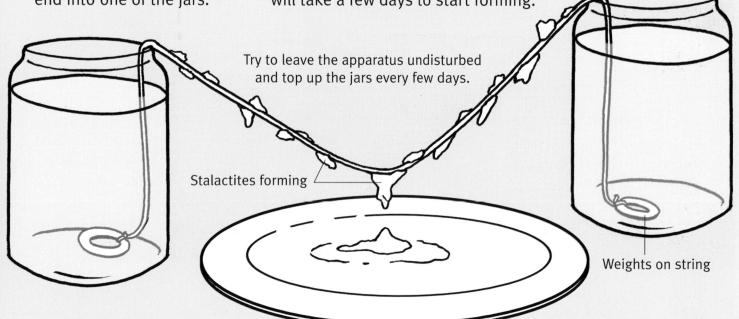

Try to leave the apparatus undisturbed and top up the jars every few days.

Stalactites forming

Weights on string

Trail Teaser

Tintin has discovered some mysterious underground wires in Dr Muller's garden. Follow the wires to see where they lead him.

(Answer on page 68)

Beastly Blunder

In the heat of battle with the beast of the Black Island, the order of events has got all muddled up. Can you put the frames back in the right order?

(Check your answer on page 68)

Flight 714 to Sydney

TINTIN AND HIS FRIENDS have been invited to the International Astronautical Congress in Sydney, Australia, to talk about their fantastic journey to the Moon in Professor Calculus's rocket. Their plane, Flight 714, just landed at Djakarta, on the island of Java. This is the last stopover before Sydney.

Captain Haddock gets off first, followed by Professor Calculus, who is always a little distracted... And here are Tintin and Snowy. For once, Snowy is on a leash, which he does not like one bit!

At the stopover on Java, the travellers bump into Laszlo Carreidas, an unusual character who has been nicknamed "the millionaire who never laughs".

Amazingly, his first conversation with Professor Calculus (or, rather, attempt at a conversation) actually cheers him up! The Professor's muddle-headed answers trigger a previously unknown phenomenon: Carreidas's laughter!

Since the millionaire is also going to Sydney, he decides that his new friends should travel with him on his private jet: the Carreidas 160.

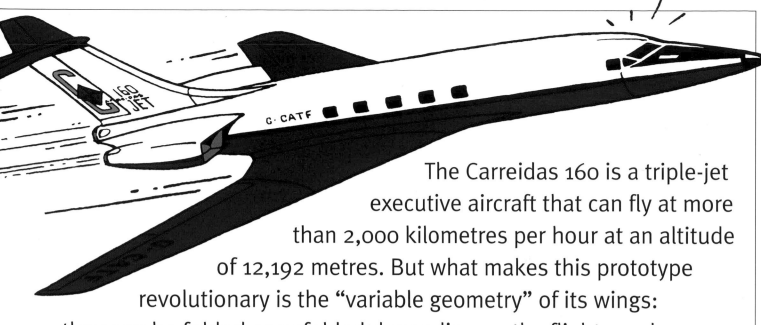

The Carreidas 160 is a triple-jet executive aircraft that can fly at more than 2,000 kilometres per hour at an altitude of 12,192 metres. But what makes this prototype revolutionary is the "variable geometry" of its wings: they can be folded or unfolded depending on the flight needs.

Carreidas's secretary, a tall, thin man with red hair called Mr Spalding, was ordered to look after his boss's new guests. Before he left the airport, Spalding did a strange thing: he made a secret phone call. He alerted his "Chief" to the presence of Tintin and his comrades. The response was brutal: "Too late to change the orders! The plan must be executed!"

From the start of the journey, Tintin had noticed Spalding's nervousness. Suddenly, the secretary goes to the cockpit and comes back with Boehm, the radio operator. The two accomplices are armed. As they point their guns at the stunned passengers, Spalding orders: "HANDS UP, EVERYONE!"

The Carreidas 160 is flying over the ocean. Inside, Tintin, Snowy, Haddock, Calculus and Carreidas are locked up in the kitchenette, along with the loyal Zlut, the pilot, and Gino, the steward. In the cockpit, the traitors Spalding, Boehm and the co-pilot Colombani have taken over the plane. The craft flies low over the waves in order to evade any control tower radars. Eventually, the Isle of Pulau-Pulau Bompa comes into view – the rendezvous point arranged by the leader of the gang.

Landing on the short runway, the aeroplane's brake parachute tears and the wheels on the undercarriage explode. Only a powerful net at the end of the landing strip stops the plane in time.

The passengers experience every terrifying bump and jolt of the sudden landing. As soon as the doors open, Snowy flees, howling in terror. Despite all this, they are alive ...

But what fate awaits the prisoners?

An uncertain fate, surely, as the prisoners realise they have fallen into the hands of Tintin's fearsome enemy ... a man whose sinister sniggering is instantly recognisable ... a wicked individual who is none other than ...

Rastapopoulos! And beside him stands an old scoundrel that Captain Haddock once commanded during the famous affair of the Crab with the Golden Claws – Allan, formerly lieutenant of Haddock's ship, the Karaboudjan.

Blowing cigar smoke in Mr Carreidas's face, Rastapopoulos reveals his reason for commanding Spalding to hijack the millionaire's plane and kidnap its passengers. It is simply a matter of forcing Carreidas to hand over his secret bank account number in order to seize his fortune.

But Lazlo Carreidas is a fighter. "You can torture me," he fumes, "rip off my nails, roast me over a slow fire or tickle my feet, I WILL NOT TALK!"

Rastapopoulos's accomplice, the corrupt Dr Krollspell, gives Mr Carreidas a truth serum injection. But the result is not what Rastapopoulos expected. Instead of revealing his account number, the millionaire starts telling of his first misdeeds: how he stole a pear when he was four years old and how, later, he stole a ring from his mother. "I am," he concludes, "a true evil genius!" The experiment had completely failed.

Meanwhile, Allan and the guards lead the prisoners to an old wartime bunker. Before closing the heavy metal door, Allan warns them, "You won't be coming out before Carreidas has talked." The wait begins…

Our friends are bored to death. Suddenly, outside the bunker, a bark: it's Snowy! Tintin's dog has found his master's trail and climbs into the bunker through a tiny window. He bites through Tintin's ropes and helps the captives overcome the guards and breathe fresh air once again.

Tintin and Captain Haddock's first task is to rescue Mr Carreidas. Quickly, they tie and gag Rastapopoulos and Krollspell. But the millionaire is being troublesome and is making the task much more difficult, so they decide to tie him up as well and seal his mouth with tape. Then they make their way to the meeting point with the other escapees.

When his captors are distracted for a brief moment, Rastapopoulos sees his chance to escape. Though his arms are tied, he runs away and joins Allan. Rastapopoulos gives his second in command a verbal lashing: "What are you waiting for?" he screams. "Follow Tintin! And don't forget Carreidas and Krollspell – I need them alive!" "Got it, boss!" replies Allan, rounding up his guards.

Meanwhile, Tintin is looking for a safe refuge for the group, when something strange happens to him. He hears a voice speaking inside his head. It tells him how to keep out of danger: "Higher … to the left … underneath the big flat rock …" Without questioning, Tintin obeys the mysterious voice. It guides him to a staircase that leads to an underground passage. Suddenly, Tintin and the others find themselves in front of an enormous statue of a human head. "Press down on the eye," whispers the voice. Then the head lifts up, revealing the entrance to a temple. To the Captain's surprise, Tintin closes the door behind him. "I locked up the entrance as I was told to do," says the young adventurer.

(Continued on page 48)

A

Technology Teaser

Many weird and wonderful machines are found throughout Tintin's adventures. Each has a particular, special function. Can you tell what all these devices are? The clues should help you.

How to Play

Read each statement carefully. Each one refers to one of the pictures. Work out which machine is which.

(Answers on page 68)

1 Look at the stars with this big magnifying glass.

2 Cuthbert's glass-shattering device is quite deadly.

3 Submarines use these to look above the water.

B

C

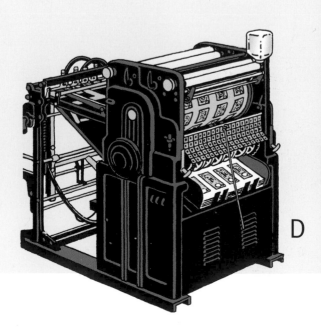

D

4 This dockside structure's arm is far stronger than yours!

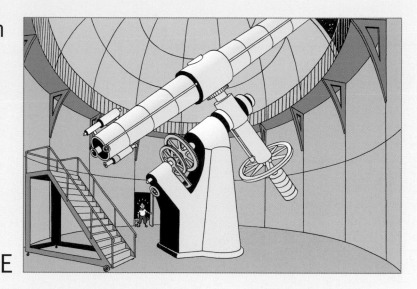

E

F

5 This enormous "ear" listens to radio signals from space.

6 This machine would be a license to print money – if it weren't illegal!

7 In olden times, sailors stored their compass inside this special box.

8 This machine shoots people, but it doesn't hurt them.

H

G

A Dog's Guide to Cats

Cats… don't you just hate them? What's that? You don't? Well, I do – after all, I'm a dog, what did you expect? Even so, I meet more types of cat than the average dog on my travels with Tintin, so I am quite an expert. Let me warn you about some of the worst kinds.

Indian Tiger

Look at this fierce beast that jumped out of the jungle while Tintin was travelling by elephant with the Maharaja (he's a very important man in India). Tigers can leap up to four metres in the air. No wonder Indians call them lords of the jungle!

Any lion that threatens Tintin runs the risk of making me angry – not a wise thing to do, as this lion found out in the Congo.

African Lion

King of the beasts? Just big pussy cats if you ask me. They're not even the biggest big cat (tigers are). OK, so they can roar like no other beast – loud enough to raise a cloud of dust or be heard eight kilometres away. But that's just showing off, right?

Leopard

When Tintin was teaching children in the Congo, a leopard came into the classroom and Tintin had to teach it a lesson. How was Tintin meant to spot that the leopard was tame?

Puma

The American wild cat is one confused kitty. It has more names than any other mammal: puma, cougar, mountain lion, Florida panther, red tiger. Imagine not even knowing for sure what you are!

Cheetah

This spotty furball thinks I gave him that bump on the head. Actually it was a falling rock, but why should I tell him that? Just don't ask me to race him – cheetahs are the fastest animals on land.

Domestic Cats

When I'm not travelling the world showing wild cats who's king of the feline world, I like to take it easy at home. But surprise, surprise: you can't even get a dog nap without some mangy moggy ruffling your fur.

You know me – bold of paw and fierce of bite. But there's a certain Siamese cat at Marlinspike who really knows how to take the wag out of my tail.

I hate it when they do that. One day, I'll climb right up after 'em, I swear!

Mountain Maze

Race along a dangerous rocky mountainside to capture the thief who has stolen King Ottakar's sceptre. Start at the arrow and travel through the gaps in the black lines until you catch the thief. Check page 68 if you get stuck!

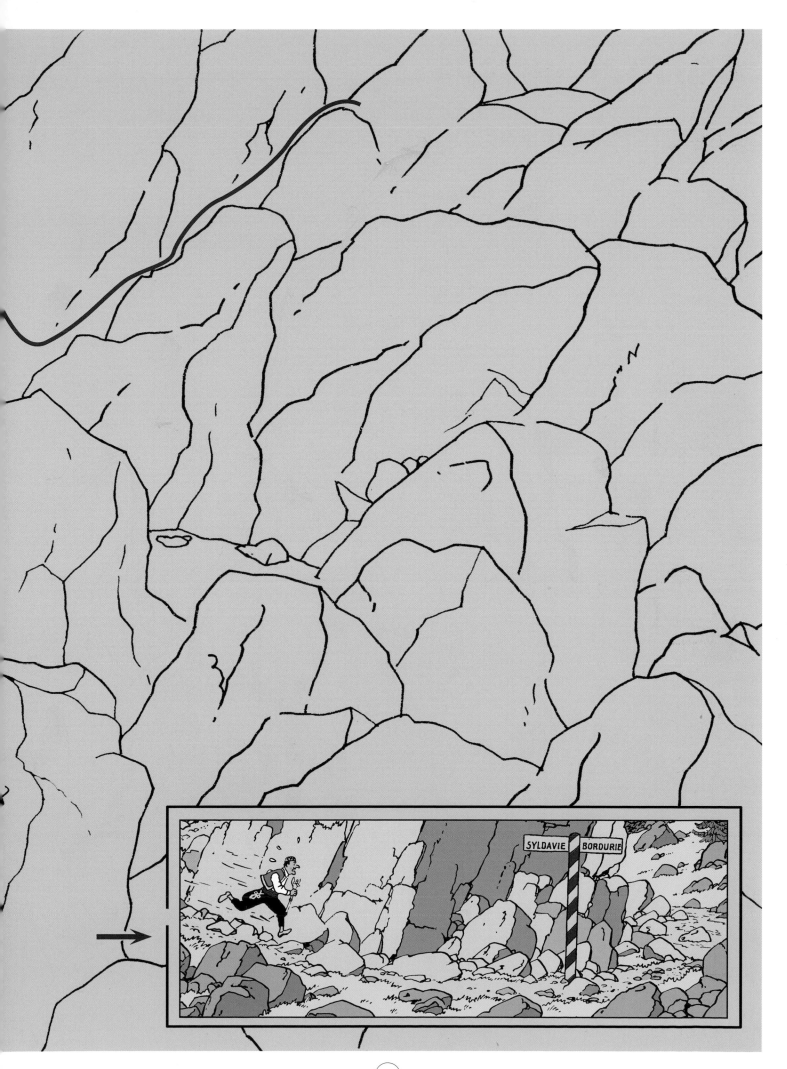

American Indians

When Tintin visits America, he meets the Blackfeet. They live in a huge area of rolling grasslands in the middle of the country called the Great Plains. The Blackfeet are just one of many North American Indian nations who live in the region.

Blackfeet

The original Blackfeet were partly nomadic, which means they travelled from place to place. Sometimes they settled and farmed the land.

Tipis

Many American Indians of the Great Plains lived in tipis. These conical tents were originally made of skins or birch bark.

Traditional Dress

The traditional dress of the Blackfeet is a jacket and leggings made of buckskin, a soft leather from the hide of deer or elk.

Feathered war bonnet worn as military dress

Tomahawk (axe)

Chief's bonnet made of eagle feathers

Chest plate made of quills

Many American Indians danced and whooped to prepare themselves for battle.

These Blackfeet are riding bareback but sometimes cloth saddles were used.

Bows

The original American Indians used bows when hunting and for warfare. Men made their own bows from wood, strung with buffalo sinew (tough fibres that connect muscles to bones).

Riding Skills

Plains Indians were superb horse riders – their modern ancestors are still proud of their riding skills, often performing at rodeos. The Comanche people, in particular, were famous for performing incredible acrobatic tricks on horseback.

Names

Traditional American Indian names often refer to animals or nature. For example, Tintin meets a chief called Keeneyed-Mole.

Reservations

An Indian reservation is land which is managed by the original nations. Today, there are about 300 Indian reservations.

Lawmakers

Tribal councils have authority over reservations.

Ceremonial smoking pipe

Know Yourself!

Tintin often pushes his body to its limits.
He chases crooks, climbs vertical cliffs,
and survives great hardships. But your body is
amazing too – and here are some eye-opening
facts to prove it!

Big Sneeze

Sneezing causes material
to shoot out of your nose
at a speed of around
150km/hour.

DID YOU KNOW?
Some people believe that we
shut our eyes when we sneeze,
because if we didn't, our eyes
would pop out of their sockets!
In fact, shutting our eyes is just
a reflex action.

Sweet Smell

Our noses recognise up to about 10,000
different smells – roses are just one of them!

DID YOU KNOW?
The ability to smell and taste go together
because odours from foods allow us
to taste more fully.

Hard Stuff

Tooth enamel is the hardest substance
in the body. Well, it has a lot of
chewing to do!

DID YOU KNOW?
Everyone has a unique tongue
print, just like a fingerprint. But
don't spread ink on your tongue to take a print.
It'll just make a mess and taste disgusting.

Night Vision

Human eyesight is surprisingly effective at night.

DID YOU KNOW?
Our eyes adjust to the dark for up to about two hours,
allowing us to see more and more.

Bawling Baby

Babies can certainly cry but their eyes don't produce tears until the baby is between three and six weeks old.

DID YOU KNOW?
We have 206 bones in our bodies. This is true for adults, but false for babies. That's because we are born with about 300 bones, but some fuse together as we grow.

Ouch!

The message that you have a pain in your foot reaches your brain almost instantaneously. The message travels up the spinal cord to the brain.

DID YOU KNOW?
There is no sense of pain within the brain itself. This is why neurosurgeons can probe areas of the brain while the patient is awake!

Keep Walking

The average person walks more than 100,000 kilometres in their lifetime – that's three times around the world! But it depends on where you live.

DID YOU KNOW?
When we walk, we use muscles in the thigh, calf and foot. But that's not all. Walking also involves muscles in the spine, hip and back. These muscles help stabilise and support us when we are moving forwards.

1

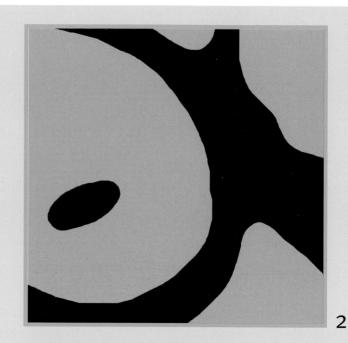

2

5

6

Lotus Enlargements

Study the large panels above.
Each one is a detail of one
of the characters from
The Blue Lotus shown below.
Can you work out who is who?

When you've reached your conclusions,
turn to page 69 to check your answers.

Wang Chen-yee   Didi Chen-yee

3

4

7

8

Mitsuhirato   J.M. Dawson   Tintin   Snowy   Chang   Rastapopoulos

45

Blue Lotus Game

Chinese painted wood furniture and house fittings are called lacquerware.

This version of the game Nine Men's Morris is inspired by the colourful Chinese designs seen in *The Blue Lotus*. Players can compete either as Tintin or as the fiendish Mitsuhiratu.

Rules of the Game

Photocopy the facing page and cut out the pieces (counters), or make your own. Each player needs nine pieces.

The basic object of the game is to make "mills" – vertical or horizontal lines of three pieces in a row. Every time a player forms a mill, that player can remove an opponent's piece from the board. The overall objective is to reduce the number of the opponent's pieces to fewer than three or render the opponent unable to play.

The game starts with the board empty. The players take turns to place their pieces on to empty intersections on the board.

After all 18 pieces have been placed, players take turns moving. A move consists of sliding a piece along one of the board lines to an adjacent intersection.

Whenever a player achieves a mill, that player immediately removes from the board one piece belonging to the opponent that does not form part of a mill. If all the opponent's pieces form mills then an exception is made and the player is allowed to remove any piece.

Captured pieces are never replayed on to the board and remain captured for the remainder of the game. The game is finished when a player loses either by being reduced to two pieces or by being unable to move.

Flight 714 to Sydney

(Continued from page 32)

IN THE TEMPLE, Tintin and consorts come across Professor Calculus, who had been led there by an extraordinary character. This unusual man introduces himself as Mik Kanrokitoff. On his head he wears some sort of antenna, which he says is a thought transmitter. He has led them, he explains, using telepathy, in order to save them from Rastapopoulos. But much more than that: he claims to be in contact with extraterrestrial beings and he is waiting here for the arrival of the next spaceship from another planet.

At this moment, an earthquake shakes the island and triggers a volcanic eruption. A torrent of lava flows into the temple. Tintin pushes his companions out of the underground passage to avoid being grilled alive.

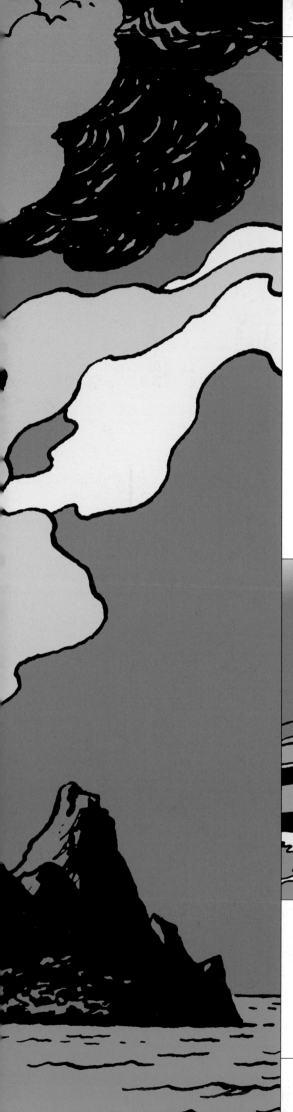

The earthquake's deadly lava flows, toxic gases and smoke were endangering the life of everyone on the island. But Tintin and his companions manage to escape the inferno, while the five members of Rastapopoulos's gang take refuge in a rubber dinghy from Carreidas's plane.

Suddenly, the spaceship appears, as Kanrokitoff had predicted. He immediately hypnotises everyone. Like unthinking robots, Tintin and his friends board the spaceship and are transported to the dinghy.

The spaceship then picks up the bandits, who are also hypnotised and incapable of resistance, and carries them off to an unknown destination …

A few hours later, one of the patrol planes sent in search of the missing Carreidas 160 flies over the waters surrounding the isle of Pulau-Pulau Bompa.

The gigantic column of smoke bellowing from the crater of the volcano makes reconnaissance difficult. But, suddenly, through a gap in the smoke, the pilot distinguishes a dot in the sea.

A little later, the control tower of Macassar receives a message: "Have located a raft with five or six men on board. No signs of life, except for a little white dog." Snowy, the only one not to be hypnotised, barks frantically towards the plane, asking to be rescued!

The plane carries the survivors back to Djakarta. The extraordinary thing is: THEY HAVE LOST ALL MEMORY of what has happened to them!

Interviewed one by one, none can give any explanation of the needle marks on the millionaire's arm, the circumstances in which the plane was diverted from its route, and, most disturbing of all, a kind of valve that Professor Calculus has found in his pocket made of a metal that DOES NOT EXIST ON EARTH!

One thing is for sure: they are expected in Australia. There they are – Tintin walking Snowy on a leash once again – calmly boarding Flight 714 to Sydney.

THE END

Carreidas 160

Wealthy tycoon Lazlo Carreidas travels the world in his supersonic executive jet, the Carreidas 160. Though it's an experimental prototype, it shares many features with other planes.

Passenger Deck

The plane provides comfortable seating for six passengers. Mr Carreidas always sits in one place, where a closed-circuit television built into his table allows him to cheat at battleships.

Rudder changes yaw
(side-to-side movement)

Mr Carreidas's company emblem of four aces

Jet engine

Turbojets

The Rolls-Royce Turbomeca turbojets deliver a total of 18,500 lbs of thrust, enabling a cruising speed at 12,000 metres of Mach 2, or over 2,000 kph.

Aircraft registration

Variable Wings

The plane uses revolutionary "variable geometry" mechanics in its wings: they can be folded or unfolded depending on the flight needs.

Flaps change lift and drag

Landing Gear

Planes use wheels, called landing gear, for taxiing, take-off, and landing. The Carreidas 160 has three sets of wheels – two main wheels and a nosewheel.

A parachute attached to the tail of the aircraft is used as a brake when landing.

Windows

Jet-plane windows are made of several layers of tough glass. At flying altitude, temperatures outside drop below freezing.

Cockpit

The plane flies with a crew consisting of a pilot, co-pilot, radio operator, navigator and steward.

Fuselage (main body)

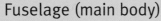
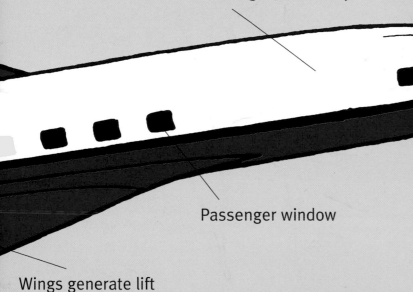

Cockpit, for command and control

Passenger window

Wings generate lift

The plane's wings move forward for maximum lift during take-off or landing, and then move to mid-position as the plane breaks the sound barrier. Finally, the wings swing right back for supersonic flight.

Radar

Aeroplanes and air traffic control use radar to stay in touch. Planes are tracked on the ground and in the air, and also guided in for smooth landings.

Radar antennae beam a radar wave to an aircraft, which bounces back to give the plane's position, direction and speed.

Ready to Land

Landing gear wheels extend on hydraulic arms from small flaps in the body of the plane just before landing.

Creative Climbing

If you use the grid, drawing your own Captain Haddock needn't be as hard as climbing a mountain. Tip: start at the bottom and work your way up. And whatever you do – don't let go (of your pencil!).

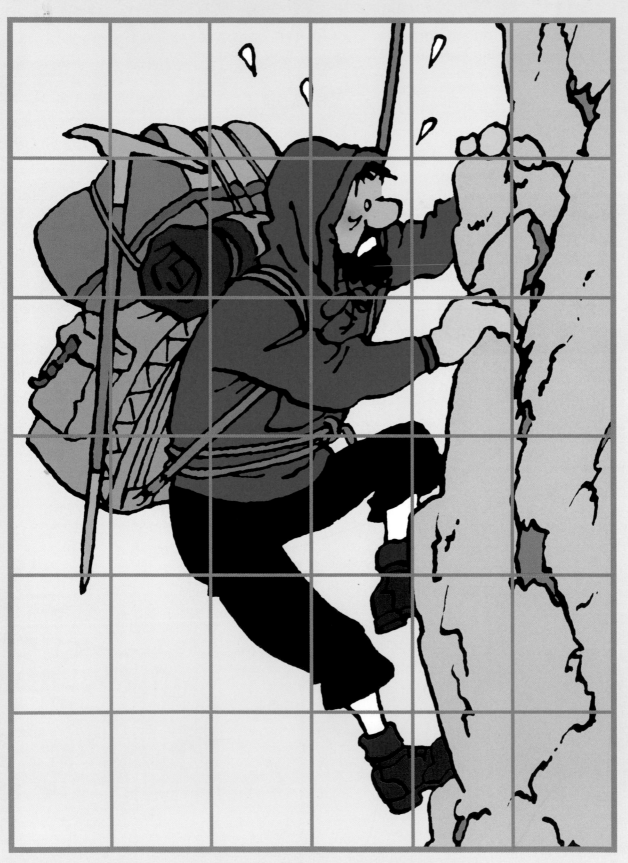

To Be Precise

A great detective must have an eye and ear for detail. It's part of the job. Thomson and Thompson are no exception. They like to get things right. Whenever one of them says something, the other rephrases it a little bit more precisely. Yet, somehow, it sounds all confused. To be precise, the Thom(p)sons are very confused.

Each quote is the 'precise' rephrasing of something the other detective has just said. But what was just said? Choose from A, B or C.

Check your answers on page 69 to see how well you did.

1 A Thomson with a straight face looks like death!

A A Thompson with a face looks straight!
B A Thompson looks death straight in the face!
C A Thompson dies with a straight face!

2 We know nothing in our job.

A You forget, my friend, in our job, there's nothing we don't know.
B Our job is to know nothing.
C No one knows our job like us.

3 If my name's Thomson we won't get far!

A The name Thompson won't go far!
B We won't get Thomson as a name!
C He won't get far, if my name's Thompson!

4 We can deny that we're ever right.

A We can't deny that we're right as ever.
B We can't be right.
C We're denied our rights.

5 We'd completely lost face!

A What a face you have!
B Time to about face!
C What a surprise to see your face again!

6 You'll see we pay for this!

A Would you like to pay for this?
B We'll see you pay for this!
C See us pay for this!

SCORE (out of 6):

0 Dumbs the word
I'd keep mum about your score
if I were you.

1–2 Not bad
To be precise, not all that good either.

3–4 Good result
Looks like you've got an ear for detail.

5–6 Perfect
Your knowledge is truly precise. Well done!

One of the Rumbaba people shows off his shrunken head collection in *The Broken Ear*.

Shrunken Heads

On the trail of a stolen statue in South America, Tintin is captured by the fierce Rumbaba people. They cut off the heads of their enemies and shrink them to the size of a fist, using a special process. These shrunken heads are then worn or displayed on tall poles as trophies.

You Will Need

- A large apple
- A lollypop stick
- A vegetable peeler
- About two metres of brown wool
- A pencil

1 Ask an adult to peel the apple for you.

2 Draw a simple face on the apple with the pencil. Use the drawing above as a guide.

3 Use the lollypop stick to carve out the features. Cut out the eye sockets, leaving the nose sticking out. Then carve out the mouth and bottom lip.

4 Now poke holes for the eyes with the pencil. Use the lollypop stick to cut some wrinkles into the face of the apple about three millimetres deep. As the apple dries these will open up.

Each cut will be magnified after shrinking, so don't dig too deep.

5 Cut the wool into 10-centimetre lengths. Tie the lengths together at one end.

6 To add hair to the head, make a hole at the top of the apple and push the knotted end of the wool into it. Shape the hair around the head.

7 Leave the apple head outside in a dry place. Within days, the apple will shrivel up and turn brown.

You could hang up your head to dry, using a string passed through the middle.

Display your shrunken head on the lollypop stick – gruesome!

Ready for Action

Tintin's life is one of sudden, unexpected adventure. Most often, he has no choice but to leap into action without a thought for whether he's properly dressed or equipped with the right tools for the job. But occasionally he has time to prepare. Here's a guide to some of the specialised equipment he uses.

When Tintin is in South America rescuing Calculus, he wears a poncho, which he uses as a sling to carry Snowy over a waterfall.

Moon Suit

When he explored the Moon, Tintin wore a spacesuit designed by Professor Calculus. It protects Tintin from the crushing vacuum of space and from the extremes of temperature on the Moon.

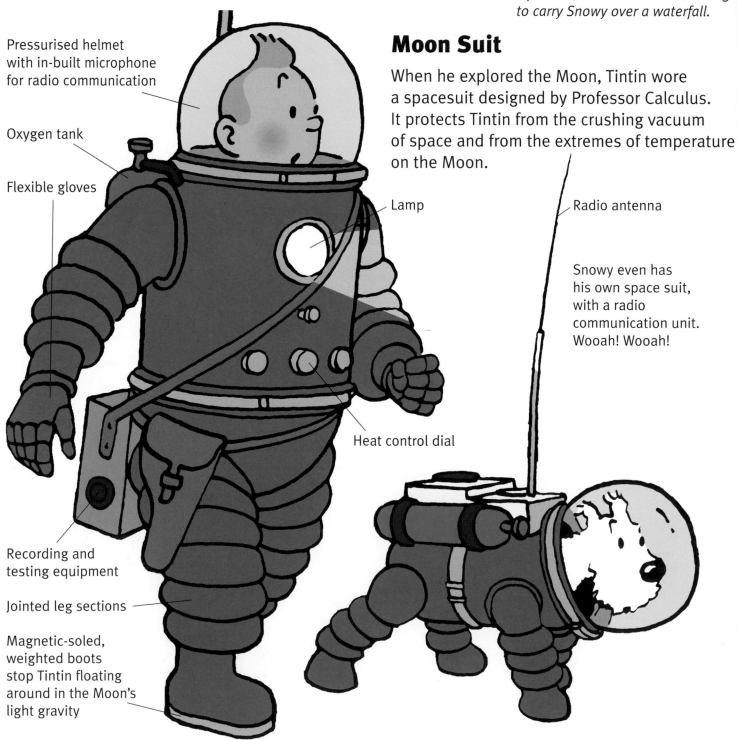

Pressurised helmet with in-built microphone for radio communication

Oxygen tank

Flexible gloves

Lamp

Radio antenna

Snowy even has his own space suit, with a radio communication unit. Wooah! Wooah!

Heat control dial

Recording and testing equipment

Jointed leg sections

Magnetic-soled, weighted boots stop Tintin floating around in the Moon's light gravity

Unneeded air escapes from one-way valve

Diving Suit

To explore the seabed in search of Red Rackham's treasure, Tintin dons a diving suit. The oxygen supply is pumped by hand from on board the ship and the only communication Tintin has with the ship is to tug on a rope.

Air-filled helmet allows Tintin to breathe under water

Glass viewing hatch opens on hinges

Oxygen supply hose

Communication rope

Tight wrist seals prevent water entering diving suit

Waterproof suit

Flag of the European Foundation for Scientific Research

Weighted boots

Fur-lined hat

Ear holes allow communication headset to be worn over the top of cap

Arctic Outfit

When Tintin goes in search of a meteorite that crash-landed in the Arctic Ocean, he has to parachute down from an aircraft on to the rock. He wears a fur-lined flight suit with a parachute attached.

Parachute harness

Fur-lined boots

Parachute cords

Car Chaos

It's market day in a small Swiss village. Shopkeepers are displaying their fruit and veg, a rug seller is setting up his stall, while farmers bring their prize animals to sell. Suddenly, without warning, Tintin and Haddock cause chaos in a speeding car, chasing a gang of kidnappers!

Look at the picture carefully for 30 seconds, then cover it, turn the page upside down and answer as many of the questions as you can. The answers are on page 69.

Questions

1 Name four kinds of animal in the picture.

2 What colour is Tintin and Haddock's car?

3 What kind of food is wrapped around the bonnet of Tintin and Haddock's car?

4 What kind of statue stands in the square?

5 What floor furnishings were being sold?

6 What has fallen out of the back of the horse and cart?

Draw a Classic Racing Car

In India, Tintin drives one of the Maharaja's racing cars in pursuit of some kidnappers. These classic sports cars are great fun to draw, with their curved lines, bright colours and period stylings.

1 Lightly draw a guideline in pencil. It should slant downwards a little bit. Draw the rear wheel sitting on the guide line. You could use a compass or find a circular object to draw round.

Use the rear wheel to measure out the distance to the front wheel. They should be just over two wheels apart.

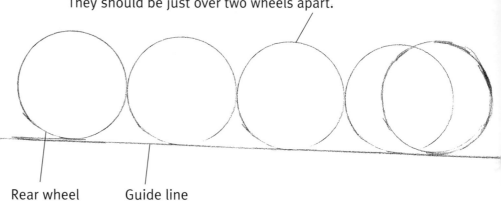

Rear wheel   Guide line

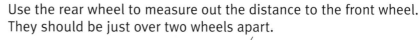

2 Draw the basic body lines. First, the bottom of the car. Then, the line of the exhaust pipe and lastly the highest point of the car body.

3 Sketch in the basic body shapes. Complete the overall shape of the car, then add the other wheels to give the sketch more definition.

Don't worry about the seating well for now.

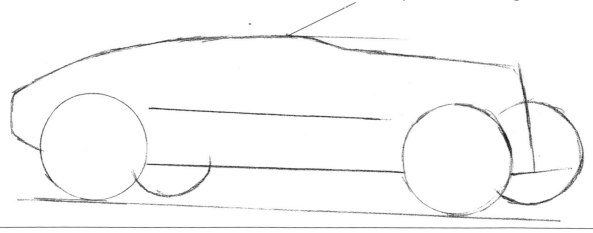

4 Mark out the side panels and the engine grille. Add the seating well and exhaust. Shape the front of the car including the bumper. Add the hubcaps – paying great attention to get these in the correct position.

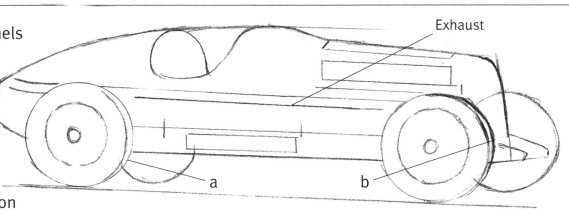

Exhaust

a   b

Give the wheels some depth. The rear wheel is a tiny bit smaller than the front, so draw the depth line (a) inside the rear wheel. On the front wheel, draw the depth line (b) outside the wheel.

5 Add more detail to the seating well, exhaust, panelling and hubcaps. Add the windscreen. Use an eraser to get rid of any unwanted lines.

6 Draw in the grilles, suspension brackets and petrol cap. Define the front radiator. Shade in some areas, so you can see if it looks correct before inking in the pencil lines.

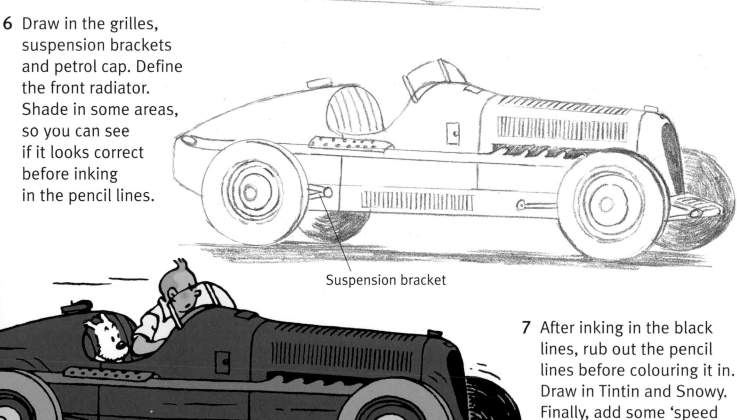

Suspension bracket

7 After inking in the black lines, rub out the pencil lines before colouring it in. Draw in Tintin and Snowy. Finally, add some 'speed lines' to make it look dynamic.

Answers

The Tintin Test
(pages 14–15)

Part 1: Tintin
1. **B** 2. **C** (in *The Shooting Star*)
3. **C**

Part 2: Snowy
1. **C** 2. **A** 3. **B** 4. **B**
(a dinosaur bone, in
King Ottokar's Sceptre)

Part 3: Crooks in America
1. **A** 2. **C** 3. **C** 4. **D**
(He's a private detective
in *Tintin in America*)

Part 4: Transport
1. **C** 2. **C** 3. **C** 4. **A**

Animals and Owners
(page 16)

The shopkeeper has a fish;
the captain has a cat;
Max has a dog;
Alonso has a parrot.

Jungle Jumble
(page 17)

```
G O S P O R E S T I H
C A R N I V A L A T A
A L T H O J E W S H D
L P S S I W B A M O D
C X E J P M Y L N M O
U T P G T O Y C U P C
L I D E G Y N A P S K
U N L Q U Y E Z Y O N
S T A P I O C A R N W
T I R E J F W R A S C
E N M J U N G L E W E
C A S T A F I O R E P
```

Signalling Flags
(pages 18–19)

1. **ZL** 2. **GW** 3. **SO** 4. **AC**

Trail Teaser
(page 24)

The wire leads
to the tree.

Beastly Blunder
(page 25)

The correct order is
8, 3, 2, 9, 6, 5, 4, 1, 7

Technology Teaser
(pages 34–35)

1. **E** (telescope)
2. **G** (ultrasonic machine)
3. **H** (periscope)
4. **A** (crane)
5. **B** (radar dish)
6. **D** (counterfeiting machine)
7. **F** (compass binnacle)
8. **C** (camera)

Mountain Maze
(pages 38–39)

Lotus Enlargements
(pages 44–45)

1. Snowy
2. Mitsuhirato
3. Tintin
4. Didi Chen-yee
5. Rastapopoulos
6. Chang
7. Wang Chen-yee
8. J.M. Dawson

To Be Precise
(pages 58–59)

1. **B** 2. **A** 3. **C** 4. **A** 5. **C** 6. **B**

Car Chaos
(pages 64–65)

1. Horse, pig, cow, dog, cat, chicken, duck, bird
2. Russet/reddish-brown
3. Sausages
4. War memorial
5. Rugs
6. Milk churns